HEART TRAINING LOG

DST

by Sally Edwards

Library of Congress Cataloging-in-Publication Data
Edwards, Sally 1947-
Heart Zones Training Log by Sally Edwards.

Includes bibliographical reference (p.) and index.
Self-Help. 2. Sports 3. Health. 4. Fitness. 5. Psychology 6. Heart Rate Monitor 7. Diary

ISBN 0-9700130-3-5

Heart Zones© Publishing

Printed in the United State of America

MSRP: $14.95 USA
Heart Zones USA
2636 Fulton Avenue • Suite 100
Sacramento, California 95821 USA
www.heartzones.com   staff@heartzones.com

TABLE OF
CONTENTS

YOUR PERSONAL
INFORMATION

Property of: _____

Address: _____

City: _____

State: _____ Zip Code: _____

E-Mail Address: _____

Starting Date: _____

Log # _____ and/or Dates from: _____ to: _____

Club: _____

Team: _____

Coach: _____

Date of Birth: _____

Sport-Specific Maximum Heart Rates

Swim: _____ bpm

Bike: _____ bpm

Run: _____ bpm

Other: _____ bpm

Other: _____ bpm

INTRODUCTION
by Sally Edwards

This is my promise to you: You'll save time and get more out of every minute of physical activity if you use this log. It helps you see if your training program is working and if you are accomplishing your goals. For the past 30 years of training and racing, I have always used a log as a key part of my success in sports. You will find it to be a great tool in your training as well.

This is a dual-purpose log. As you record your information, this diary will serve as a motivational tool. It will show you if your actual training and your training plan truly match each other. Second, this log is a permanent record for you to look back on when you are planning ahead to achieve your next goal. By recording the how, when, what, how long, how hard, and how much, you will be able to maximize your workouts and fine tune your program, eliminating certain workouts and parts of workouts that don't help you achieve your goals.

You'll develop your own analysis of this information as you grow to love the process. For example, I love to look at averages - average workout times, average heart rates, and average speed. I like "averages" because they help assess improvement.

It takes less than five minutes a day to fill out your log. The information you record can be used for a lifetime so it's worth the brief time required. Your log also makes you the author of your exercise program. A well-kept log is far superior to depending on sheer memory when you want to recall a training period. Let your log become your friend, consultant, and diary. Share it with those who support and help you be successful by asking them for their evaluation of the information in it.

One of my favorite sayings is "When was the last time you did something for the first time?" If a log is a first time tool, enjoy exploring what it can provide for you. You'll never go back.

Sally Edwards
athlete, author, speaker, training expert

To contact Sally:

Heart Zones
2636 Fulton Ave, Suite 100
Sacramento, CA 95821, USA
Phone: 916-481-7283
Fax: 916-481-2213
web: www.HeartZones.com
email: Staff@HeartZone.com

My special appreciation to the following people who made this log possible:

Page Layout: www.alanjsilva.net
Cover Design: Gina Barbosa
Proof Readers & Consultants: Ellen Sampson & Carla Felstadt

NOTE It's wonderful that sport and training are the same. But, our spelling is sometimes different. This logbook was written in American English. Please enjoy both and accept our spelling differences.

COMPLETING YOUR
LOG PAGE

 Date: This is for the month, date and day of week.

 Sport Activity: List each sport activity for the day.

 DST **Distance/Time**: Record the distance and elapsed time of each activity.

 Heart Zone Number and Time In Zone: Enter the heart zone(s), and the amount of time you spent in each of them. If you would like more information about this system, see the list of resources at the end of this book.

Key Workout Type: There are basically three key workouts
1. **Speed:** (SP) also known as tempo (TE), intervals (IN) or time trials (TT)
2. **Endurance:** (EN) also known as steady state, easy intensity or long slow distance (LSD)
3. **Strength:** (ST) also known as "hill training"

Average: Record your average heart rate, average bike or running speed, or other relevant averages. You can easily calculate your speed averages by dividing distance by time.

am Heart Rate: Record your morning heart rate.

Weight Training Time: Enter your time spent doing resistance or weight training.

Stretching Time: Record the minutes spent in stretching activity.

Recovery Heart Rate: Record the number of heart-beats you drop in one minute.

Body Weight/Fat %: Enter your body weight and or your percent body fat.

A, B, C, F

Rating: This is a subjective evaluation of your "feelings" about the workout. Use letter grades, such as an "A" for the best grade, when your training time was well spent, and a poorer grade, say a "C⁺", if the workout started poorly but got better as it concluded.

$\sum_{HZT}$

Total Heart Zone Training Points: This is the cardiac weight of the workout. To calculate points, multiple the heart zone number by the number of minutes spent in that heart zone.

Example:

20 minutes in Zone 2	=	40 HZT Points
15 minutes in Zone 3	=	45 HZT Points
Total HZT Points		**= 85 HZT Points**

HEART ZONES TRAINING — MAXIMUM HEART RATE

HEART ZONES TRAINING

Training Zone (% maximum heart rate)	Fuel Burned	Max HR 160	Max HR 165	Max HR 170	Max HR 175	Max HR 180	Max HR 185	Max HR 190	Max HR 195	Max HR 200	Max HR 205	Max HR 210	Max HR 215	Max HR 220	Max HR 225	Max HR 230	Max HR 235	Max HR 240
Z5 RED LINE 90%-100%	PROTEIN →	160	165	170	175	180	185	190	195	200	205	210	215	220	225	230	235	240
		144	149	153	158	162	167	171	176	180	185	189	194	198	203	207	211	216
Z4 THRESHOLD 80%-90%		144	149	153	158	162	167	171	176	180	185	189	194	198	203	207	211	216
	CARBOHYDRATES	128	132	136	140	144	148	152	156	160	164	168	172	176	180	184	188	192
Z3 AEROBIC 70%-80%		128	132	136	140	144	148	152	156	160	164	168	172	176	180	184	188	192
		112	116	119	123	126	130	133	137	140	143	147	151	154	158	164	165	168
Z2 TEMPERATE 60%-70%		112	116	119	123	126	130	133	137	140	143	147	151	154	158	164	165	168
	FAT	96	99	102	105	108	111	114	117	120	123	126	129	132	135	138	141	144
Z1 HEALTHY HEART		96	99	102	105	108	111	114	117	120	123	126	129	132	135	138	141	144
		80	83	85	88	90	93	95	98	100	103	105	108	110	113	115	118	120

HOW TO USE THE MAXIMUM
HEART RATE CHART

5 Steps to Better Fitness and Performance:

1. **Choose your Heart Zone:** Select one of the five different training zones based on the exercise goals for your workout.

2. **Set your Maximum Heart Rate:** Find your maximum heart rate (Max HR) around the outer edge of the chart.

3. **Determine your Training Zone:** The shaded area where your selected training zone and Max HR column intersect is your heart rate training zone.

4. **Set the Zone:** The lower heart rate number in the shaded area is the floor of your training zone and the upper number is the ceiling.

5. **Stay in the Zone:** During each workout, maintain your heart rate between your zone floor and ceiling (excluding warm up and cool down).

SAMPLE COMPLETED
LOG PAGE

Date	Sport Activity	DST Distance	Time	Z1	Z2	Z3	Z4	Z5
3/15	Swim	1000	30min	3min	15min	12min	–	–
3/16	Run	8mi	1:30	–	10min	60min	–	–
	Swim	1500	1:00	6min	30min	30min	–	–
3/17	Rest Day							
3/18	Bike	18mi	1:15	–	9min	41min	25min	6min
3/19	Run	5mi	45min	10min	12min	28min	–	–
3/20	Bike	20mi	1:15	–	15min	60min	–	–
3/21	Run	6mi	55min	–	15min	30min	10min	–

Time In Zone

	Total Training Time (min):			Z1	Z2	Z3	Z4	Z5
Summary for the Week		427		19	106	261	35	6
				1 %	24 %	62 %	8 %	1 %
Year-to-Date Summary	Total Training Time (min):	2,555		185	269	1229	642	230
				7 %	10 %	48 %	25 %	9 %

Notes: I am really enjoying this training period. The feeling of getting fitter is wonderful!

Key Workout Type	Averages	am Heart Rate	Body Weight/ Fat	Recovery Heart Rate	Weight Training Time	Stretching Time	A, B, C, F Training Rating	Σ HZT HZT Points
durance	150	62	167	24	–	15min	B	69
durance	174			36				200
peed	158	61	169	34	–	20min	B	240
ength	160	62	168	35	30min	20min	B+	271
durance	140	–	–		–	–	A	118
durance	145	63	168	26	45min	20min	A	210
eed	170	60	167		15min	20min	A	250
A V E R A G E O R T O T A L S	154	61.6	167	31	1:30	1:35	B+	1211
		BPM	LBS.	BPM	MIN.	MIN.	RATING	

es: Wish I had more time because I'd like to stretch more. I did stretch 5 x this week!

Date	Sport Activity	DST Distance	Time	Time In Zone				
				Z1	Z2	Z3	Z4	Z5
8/27	STRENGTH (SM)		1:15					
8/28	SWIM (E-FORM)		:45					

Summary for the Week	Total Training Time (min):	Z1	Z2	Z3	Z4	Z5
		%	%	%	%	%

Year-to-Date Summary	Total Training Time (min):	Z1	Z2	Z3	Z4	Z5
		%	%	%	%	%

Notes:

Key rkout ype	Averages	am Heart Rate	Body Weight/ Fat	Recovery Heart Rate	Weight Training Time	Stretching Time	A, B, C, F Training Rating	Σ HZT HZT Points
		A V E R A G E O R T O T A L S						
		BPM	LBS.	BPM	MIN.	MIN.	RATING	

s:

YEAR: _____

Date	Sport Activity	DST Distance	Time	Z1	Z2	Z3	Z4	Z5

Time In Zone

Summary for the Week	Total Training Time (min):			Z1	Z2	Z3	Z4	Z5
					%	%	%	%

Year-to-Date Summary	Total Training Time (min):			Z1	Z2	Z3	Z4	Z5
					%	%	%	%

Notes:

Key Workout Type	Averages	am Heart Rate	Body Weight/ Fat	Recovery Heart Rate	Weight Training Time	Stretching Time	A, B, C, F Training Rating	Σ HZT HZT Points
		AVERAGE OR TOTALS						
		BPM	LBS.	BPM	MIN.	MIN.	RATING	

Notes:

Date	Sport Activity	DST Distance	Time	Time In Zone				
				Z1	Z2	Z3	Z4	Z5
Summary for the Week	**Total Training Time (min):**			Z1	Z2	Z3	Z4	Z5
				%	%	%	%	%
Year-to-Date Summary	**Total Training Time (min):**			Z1	Z2	Z3	Z4	Z5
				%	%	%	%	%

Notes:

Key Workout Type	Averages	am Heart Rate	Body Weight/ Fat	Recovery Heart Rate	Weight Training Time	STRETCH Stretching Time	A, B, C, F Training Rating	Σ HZT HZT Points
		A V E R A G E O R T O T A L S						
		BPM	LBS.	BPM	MIN.	MIN.	RATING	

Notes:

WEEK 4 OF LOG PAGES

YEAR: _____

Date	Sport Activity	DST Distance	Time	Z1	Time In Zone Z2	Z3	Z4	Z5
Summary for the Week	Total Training Time (min):			Z1	Z2	Z3	Z4	Z5
				%	%	%	%	%
Year-to-Date Summary	Total Training Time (min):			Z1	Z2	Z3	Z4	Z5
				%	%	%	%	%

Notes:

Key Workout Type	Averages	am Heart Rate	Body Weight/ Fat	Recovery Heart Rate	Weight Training Time	Stretching Time	A, B, C, F Training Rating	Σ HZT HZT Points
		AVERAGE		OR		TOTALS		
		BPM	LBS.	BPM	MIN.	MIN.	RATING	

otes:

4 WEEK BLOCK
SUMMARY

4 Week Block: 1	Total Year-to-Date
Sport:	
Sport:	
Sport:	

Total Distance: _____ Year-to-Date _____

Total Time: _____ Year-to-Date _____

# of Key Workouts: _____ Year-to-Date _____

Total Time in Each Heart Zone:

• Zone 1 Healthy Heart _____

• Zone 2 Temperate_____

• Zone 3 Aerobic _____

• Zone 4 Threshold _____

• Zone 5 Red Line _____

Goals Accomplished This Month:

1. _____

2. _____

3. _____

4. _____

Goals to be Accomplished Next Month:

1. _____

2. _____

3. _____

4. _____

4 WEEK BLOCK
SUMMARY

Comments about my physical condition:

_____

_____

_____

_____

Comments about my mental condition:

_____

_____

_____

_____

Comments about my overall training:

_____

_____

_____

_____

Date	Sport Activity	DST Distance	Time	Z1	Z2	Z3	Z4	Z5

				Z1	Z2	Z3	Z4	Z5
Summary for the Week	Total Training Time (min):							
				%	%	%	%	%
Year-to-Date Summary	Total Training Time (min):			Z1	Z2	Z3	Z4	Z5
				%	%	%	%	%

Notes:

Key Workout Type	Averages	am Heart Rate	Body Weight/ Fat	Recovery Heart Rate	Weight Training Time	Stretching Time	A, B, C, F Training Rating	HZT Points
		AVERAGE OR TOTALS						
		BPM	LBS.	BPM	MIN.	MIN.	RATING	

Notes:

Date	Sport Activity	DST Distance	Time	Time In Zone Z1	Z2	Z3	Z4	Z5
Summary for the Week	**Total Training Time (min):**			Z1	Z2	Z3	Z4	Z5
				%	%	%	%	%
Year-to-Date Summary	**Total Training Time (min):**			Z1	Z2	Z3	Z4	Z5
				%	%	%	%	%

Notes:

Key Workout Type	♥ Averages	♥am am Heart Rate	Body Weight/ Fat	↓♥ Recovery Heart Rate	T Weight Training Time	STRETCH Stretching Time	A, B, C, F Training Rating	Σ HZT HZT Points
			A V E R A G E O R T O T A L S					
		BPM	LBS.	BPM	MIN.	MIN.	RATING	

Notes:

WEEK 7 OF LOG PAGES

YEAR: _____

Date	Sport Activity	DST Distance	Time	Time In Zone Z1	Z2	Z3	Z4	Z5
Summary for the Week	Total Training Time (min):			Z1	Z2	Z3	Z4	Z5
				%	%	%	%	%
Year-to-Date Summary	Total Training Time (min):			Z1	Z2	Z3	Z4	Z5
				%	%	%	%	%

Notes:

Key Workout Type	Averages	am Heart Rate	Body Weight/ Fat	Recovery Heart Rate	Weight Training Time	Stretching Time	A, B, C, F Training Rating	Σ HZT HZT Points
	AVERAGE OR TOTALS							
		BPM	LBS.	BPM	MIN.	MIN.	RATING	

Notes:

Date	Sport Activity	DST Distance	Time	Time In Zone Z1	Z2	Z3	Z4	Z5
Summary for the Week	Total Training Time (min):			Z1	Z2	Z3	Z4	Z5
				%	%	%	%	
Year-to-Date Summary	Total Training Time (min):			Z1	Z2	Z3	Z4	Z5
				%	%	%	%	

Notes:

Key Workout Type	Averages	am Heart Rate	Body Weight/ Fat	Recovery Heart Rate	Weight Training Time	STRETCH Stretching Time	A, B, C, F Training Rating	Σ HZT HZT Points
		A V E R A G E O R T O T A L S						
		BPM	LBS.	BPM	MIN.	MIN.	RATING	

otes:

4 WEEK BLOCK
SUMMARY

4 Week Block: 2	Total Year-to-Date
Sport:	
Sport:	
Sport:	

Total Distance: _____ Year-to-Date _____

Total Time: _____ Year-to-Date _____

# of Key Workouts: _____ Year-to-Date _____

Total Time in Each Heart Zone:

• Zone 1 Healthy Heart _____

• Zone 2 Temperate _____

• Zone 3 Aerobic _____

• Zone 4 Threshold _____

• Zone 5 Red Line _____

Goals Accomplished This Month:

1. _____

2. _____

3. _____

4. _____

Goals to be Accomplished Next Month:

1. _____

2. _____

3. _____

4. _____

4 WEEK BLOCK
SUMMARY

Comments about my physical training:

_____

_____

_____

_____

Comments about my emotional training:

_____

_____

_____

_____

Comments about my overall training:

_____

_____

_____

_____

www.HeartZones.co

YEAR: _____

Date	Sport Activity	DST Distance	Time	Z1	Z2	Z3	Z4	Z5

		Z1	Z2	Z3	Z4	Z5
Summary for the Week	Total Training Time (min):					
		%	%	%	%	%
Year-to-Date Summary	Total Training Time (min):	Z1	Z2	Z3	Z4	Z5
		%	%	%	%	%

Notes:

Key Workout Type	Averages	am Heart Rate	Body Weight/ Fat	Recovery Heart Rate	Weight Training Time	STRETCH Stretching Time	A, B, C, F Training Rating	Σ HZT HZT Points
		A V E R A G E O R T O T A L S						
		BPM	LBS.	BPM	MIN.	MIN.	RATING	

tes:

Date	Sport Activity	DST Distance	Time	Z1	Z2	Z3	Z4	Z5
Summary for the Week	Total Training Time (min):			Z1	Z2	Z3	Z4	Z5
				%	%	%	%	
Year-to-Date Summary	Total Training Time (min):			Z1	Z2	Z3	Z4	Z5
				%	%	%	%	

Notes:

Key Workout Type	Averages	am Heart Rate	Body Weight/ Fat	Recovery Heart Rate	Weight Training Time	Stretching Time	A, B, C, F Training Rating	Σ HZT HZT Points
		A V E R A G E O R T O T A L S						
		BPM	LBS.	BPM	MIN.	MIN.	RATING	

tes:

YEAR: _____

Date	Sport Activity	DST Distance	⏱ Time	Time In Zone Z1	Z2	Z3	Z4	Z5
Summary for the Week	**Total Training Time (min):**			Z1	Z2	Z3	Z4	Z5
				%	%	%	%	
Year-to-Date Summary	**Total Training Time (min):**			Z1	Z2	Z3	Z4	Z5
				%	%	%	%	

Notes:

Key Workout Type	Averages	am Heart Rate	Body Weight/ Fat	Recovery Heart Rate	Weight Training Time	STRETCH Stretching Time	A, B, C, F Training Rating	Σ HZT HZT Points
	A V E R A G E O R T O T A L S							
		BPM	LBS.	BPM	MIN.	MIN.	RATING	

Notes:

Date	Sport Activity	DST Distance	Time	Time In Zone Z1	Z2	Z3	Z4	Z5

Summary for the Week	Total Training Time (min):	Z1	Z2	Z3	Z4	Z5
		%	%	%	%	
Year-to-Date Summary	Total Training Time (min):	Z1	Z2	Z3	Z4	Z5
		%	%	%	%	

Notes:

Key Workout Type	Averages	am Heart Rate	Body Weight/ Fat	Recovery Heart Rate	Weight Training Time	Stretching Time	A, B, C, F Training Rating	Σ HZT HZT Points
		A V E R A G E		O R		T O T A L S		
		BPM	LBS.	BPM	MIN.	MIN.	RATING	

tes:

4 WEEK BLOCK
SUMMARY

4 Week Block: 3	Total Year-to-Date
Sport:	
Sport:	
Sport:	

Total Distance: _____ Year-to-Date _____

Total Time: _____ Year-to-Date _____

# of Key Workouts: _____ Year-to-Date _____

Total Time in Each Heart Zone:

- Zone 1 Healthy Heart _____
- Zone 2 Temperate _____
- Zone 3 Aerobic _____
- Zone 4 Threshold _____
- Zone 5 Red Line _____

Goals Accomplished This Month:

1. _____
2. _____
3. _____
4. _____

Goals to be Accomplished Next Month:

1. _____
2. _____
3. _____
4. _____

4 WEEK BLOCK
SUMMARY

Comments about my physical training:

_____

_____

_____

_____

Comments about my emotional training:

_____

_____

_____

_____

Comments about my overall training:

_____

_____

_____

_____

Date	Sport Activity	DST Distance	Time	Time In Zone Z1	Z2	Z3	Z4	Z5

Summary for the Week	Total Training Time (min):			Z1	Z2	Z3	Z4	Z5
				%	%	%	%	
Year-to-Date Summary	Total Training Time (min):			Z1	Z2	Z3	Z4	Z5
				%	%	%	%	

Notes:

Key Workout Type	Averages	am Heart Rate	Body Weight/ Fat	Recovery Heart Rate	Weight Training Time	Stretching Time	A, B, C, F Training Rating	Σ HZT HZT Points
		A V E R A G E		O R	T O T A L S			
		BPM	LBS.	BPM	MIN.	MIN.	RATING	

Notes:

Date	Sport Activity	DST Distance	Time	Z1	Z2	Z3	Z4	Z5
Summary for the Week	Total Training Time (min):			Z1	Z2	Z3	Z4	Z5
				%	%	%	%	
Year-to-Date Summary	Total Training Time (min):			Z1	Z2	Z3	Z4	Z5
				%	%	%	%	

Notes:

Key Workout Type	Averages	am Heart Rate	Body Weight/ Fat	Recovery Heart Rate	Weight Training Time	STRETCH Stretching Time	A, B, C, F Training Rating	Σ HZT HZT Points
	AVERAGE OR TOTALS							
		BPM	LBS.	BPM	MIN.	MIN.	RATING	

tes:

WEEK 15 OF LOG PAGES

YEAR: _____

Date	Sport Activity	DST Distance	Time	Z1	Z2	Z3	Z4	Z5

Time In Zone

		Z1	Z2	Z3	Z4	Z5
Summary for the Week	Total Training Time (min):					
		%	%	%	%	
Year-to-Date Summary	Total Training Time (min):					
		%	%	%	%	

Notes:

Key Workout Type	Averages	am Heart Rate	Body Weight/ Fat	Recovery Heart Rate	Weight Training Time	STRETCH Stretching Time	A, B, C, F Training Rating	Σ HZT HZT Points
		A V E R A G E		O R		T O T A L S		
		BPM	LBS.	BPM	MIN.	MIN.	RATING	

tes:

Date	Sport Activity	DST Distance	Time	Z1	Z2	Z3	Z4	Z5

Time In Zone

				Z1	Z2	Z3	Z4	Z5
Summary for the Week	Total Training Time (min):							
				%	%	%	%	
Year-to-Date Summary	Total Training Time (min):			Z1	Z2	Z3	Z4	Z5
				%	%	%	%	

Notes:

Key Workout Type	Averages	am Heart Rate	Body Weight/ Fat	Recovery Heart Rate	Weight Training Time	Stretching Time	A, B, C, F Training Rating	Σ HZT HZT Points
		A V E R A G E O R T O T A L S						
		BPM	LBS.	BPM	MIN.	MIN.	RATING	

tes:

4 WEEK BLOCK
SUMMARY

4 Week Block: 4	Total Year-to-Date
Sport:	
Sport:	
Sport:	

Total Distance: _____ Year-to-Date _____

Total Time: _____ Year-to-Date _____

# of Key Workouts: _____ Year-to-Date _____

Total Time in Each Heart Zone:

- Zone 1 Healthy Heart _____
- Zone 2 Temperate _____
- Zone 3 Aerobic _____
- Zone 4 Threshold _____
- Zone 5 Red Line _____

Goals Accomplished This Month:

1. _____
2. _____
3. _____
4. _____

Goals to be Accomplished Next Month:

1. _____
2. _____
3. _____
4. _____

4 WEEK BLOCK
SUMMARY

Comments about my physical training:

_____

_____

_____

_____

Comments about my emotional training:

_____

_____

_____

_____

Comments about my overall training:

_____

_____

_____

_____

WEEK 17 OF LOG PAGES

YEAR: _____

Date	Sport Activity	DST Distance	Time	Z1	Z2	Z3	Z4	Z5

				Z1	Z2	Z3	Z4	Z5
Summary for the Week	Total Training Time (min):							
				%	%	%	%	
Year-to-Date Summary	Total Training Time (min):			Z1	Z2	Z3	Z4	Z5
				%	%	%	%	

Notes:

Key Workout Type	Averages	am Heart Rate	Body Weight/ Fat	Recovery Heart Rate	Weight Training Time	Stretching Time	A, B, C, F Training Rating	$\sum$ HZT HZT Points
		A V E R A G E	O R	T O T A L S				
		BPM	LBS.	BPM	MIN.	MIN.	RATING	

Notes:

Date	Sport Activity	DST Distance	Time	Time In Zone Z1	Z2	Z3	Z4	Z5

Summary for the Week	Total Training Time (min):	Z1	Z2	Z3	Z4	Z5
		%	%	%	%	

Year-to-Date Summary	Total Training Time (min):	Z1	Z2	Z3	Z4	Z5
		%	%	%	%	

Notes:

Key Workout Type	Averages	am Heart Rate	Body Weight/ Fat	Recovery Heart Rate	Weight Training Time	STRETCH Stretching Time	A, B, C, F Training Rating	Σ HZT HZT Points
	AVERAGE OR TOTALS							
		BPM	LBS.	BPM	MIN.	MIN.	RATING	

tes:

Date	Sport Activity	DST Distance	Time	Time In Zone Z1	Z2	Z3	Z4	Z5
Summary for the Week	Total Training Time (min):			Z1	Z2	Z3	Z4	Z5
					%	%	%	%
Year-to-Date Summary	Total Training Time (min):			Z1	Z2	Z3	Z4	Z5
					%	%	%	%

Notes:

Key Workout Type	Averages	am Heart Rate	Body Weight/ Fat	Recovery Heart Rate	Weight Training Time	*STRETCH* Stretching Time	A, B, C, F Training Rating	Σ HZT HZT Points
		A V E R A G E O R T O T A L S						
		BPM	LBS.	BPM	MIN.	MIN.	RATING	

Notes:

Date	Sport Activity	DST Distance	Time	Time In Zone				
				Z1	Z2	Z3	Z4	Z5

Summary for the Week	Total Training Time (min):	Z1	Z2	Z3	Z4	Z5
		%	%	%	%	

Year-to-Date Summary	Total Training Time (min):	Z1	Z2	Z3	Z4	Z5
		%	%	%	%	

Notes:

Key Workout Type	Averages	am Heart Rate	Body Weight/ Fat	Recovery Heart Rate	Weight Training Time	STRETCH Stretching Time	A, B, C, F Training Rating	Σ HZT HZT Points
		AVERAGE OR TOTALS						
		BPM	LBS.	BPM	MIN.	MIN.	RATING	

Notes:

4 WEEK BLOCK

SUMMARY

4 Week Block: 5	Total Year-to-Date
Sport:	
Sport:	
Sport:	

Total Distance: _____ Year-to-Date _____

Total Time: _____ Year-to-Date _____

# of Key Workouts: _____ Year-to-Date _____

Total Time in Each Heart Zone:

- Zone 1 Healthy Heart _____
- Zone 2 Temperate _____
- Zone 3 Aerobic _____
- Zone 4 Threshold _____
- Zone 5 Red Line _____

Goals Accomplished This Month:

1. _____
2. _____
3. _____
4. _____

Goals to be Accomplished Next Month:

1. _____
2. _____
3. _____
4. _____

4 WEEK BLOCK
SUMMARY

Comments about my physical training:

_____

_____

_____

_____

Comments about my emotional training:

_____

_____

_____

_____

Comments about my overall training:

_____

_____

_____

_____

Date	Sport Activity	DST Distance	Time	Time In Zone				
				Z1	Z2	Z3	Z4	Z5

Summary for the Week	Total Training Time (min):			Z1	Z2	Z3	Z4	Z5
				%	%	%	%	%
Year-to-Date Summary	Total Training Time (min):			Z1	Z2	Z3	Z4	Z5
				%	%	%	%	

Notes:

Key Workout Type	Averages	am Heart Rate	Body Weight/ Fat	Recovery Heart Rate	Weight Training Time	*STRETCH* Stretching Time	A, B, C, F Training Rating	Σ HZT HZT Points
			A V E R A G E O R T O T A L S					
		BPM	LBS.	BPM	MIN.	MIN.	RATING	

otes:

_____
_____
_____
_____
_____
_____
_____

WEEK 22 OF LOG PAGES

YEAR: _____

Date	Sport Activity	DST Distance	Time	Z1	Z2	Z3	Z4	Z5
Summary for the Week	Total Training Time (min):			Z1	Z2	Z3	Z4	Z5
				%	%	%	%	%
Year-to-Date Summary	Total Training Time (min):			Z1	Z2	Z3	Z4	Z5
				%	%	%	%	%

Notes:

Key Workout Type	Averages	am Heart Rate	Body Weight/ Fat	Recovery Heart Rate	Weight Training Time	Stretching Time	A, B, C, F Training Rating	Σ_{HZT} HZT Points
		A V E R A G E O R T O T A L S						
		BPM	LBS.	BPM	MIN.	MIN.	RATING	

Notes:

Date	Sport Activity	DST Distance	Time	Time In Zone				
				Z1	Z2	Z3	Z4	Z5
Summary for the Week	Total Training Time (min):			Z1	Z2	Z3	Z4	Z5
				%	%	%	%	%
Year-to-Date Summary	Total Training Time (min):			Z1	Z2	Z3	Z4	Z5
				%	%	%	%	%

Notes:

Key Workout Type	Averages	am Heart Rate	Body Weight/ Fat	Recovery Heart Rate	Weight Training Time	Stretching Time	A, B, C, F Training Rating	Σ_{HZT} HZT Points
		A V E R A G E O R T O T A L S						
		BPM	LBS.	BPM	MIN.	MIN.	RATING	

Notes:

Date	Sport Activity	DST Distance	Time	Time In Zone Z1	Z2	Z3	Z4	Z5
Summary for the Week	Total Training Time (min):			Z1	Z2	Z3	Z4	Z5
				%	%	%	%	%
Year-to-Date Summary	Total Training Time (min):			Z1	Z2	Z3	Z4	Z5
				%	%	%	%	%

Notes:

Key Workout Type	Averages	am Heart Rate	Body Weight/ Fat	Recovery Heart Rate	Weight Training Time	Stretching Time	A, B, C, F Training Rating	Σ HZT HZT Points
	AVERAGE OR TOTALS							
		BPM	LBS.	BPM	MIN.	MIN.	RATING	

Notes:

4 WEEK BLOCK
SUMMARY

4 Week Block: 6	Total Year-to-Date
Sport:	
Sport:	
Sport:	

Total Distance: _____ Year-to-Date _____

Total Time: _____ Year-to-Date _____

# of Key Workouts: _____ Year-to-Date _____

Total Time in Each Heart Zone:

• Zone 1 Healthy Heart _____

• Zone 2 Temperate _____

• Zone 3 Aerobic _____

• Zone 4 Threshold _____

• Zone 5 Red Line _____

Goals Accomplished This Month:

1. _____

2. _____

3. _____

4. _____

Goals to be Accomplished Next Month:

1. _____

2. _____

3. _____

4. _____

4 WEEK BLOCK
SUMMARY

Comments about my physical training:

_____

_____

_____

_____

Comments about my emotional training:

_____

_____

_____

_____

Comments about my overall training:

_____

_____

_____

_____

Date	Sport Activity	DST Distance	Time	Time In Zone				
				Z1	Z2	Z3	Z4	Z5
Summary for the Week	Total Training Time (min):			Z1	Z2	Z3	Z4	Z5
				%	%	%	%	%
Year-to-Date Summary	Total Training Time (min):			Z1	Z2	Z3	Z4	Z5
				%	%	%	%	%

Notes:

Key Workout Type	Averages	am Heart Rate	Body Weight/ Fat	Recovery Heart Rate	Weight Training Time	STRETCH Stretching Time	A, B, C, F Training Rating	Σ_{HZT} HZT Points
		A V E R A G E	O R	T O T A L S				
		BPM	LBS.	BPM	MIN.	MIN.	RATING	

Notes:

Date	Sport Activity	DST Distance	Time	Time In Zone Z1	Z2	Z3	Z4	Z5

Summary for the Week	Total Training Time (min):	Z1	Z2	Z3	Z4	Z5
		%	%	%	%	%

Year-to-Date Summary	Total Training Time (min):	Z1	Z2	Z3	Z4	Z5
		%	%	%	%	%

Notes:

Key Workout Type	Averages	am Heart Rate	Body Weight/ Fat	Recovery Heart Rate	Weight Training Time	STRETCH Stretching Time	A, B, C, F Training Rating	Σ HZT HZT Points
		A V E R A G E		O R	T O T A L S			
		BPM	LBS.	BPM	MIN.	MIN.	RATING	

Notes:

Date	Sport Activity	DST Distance	Time	Z1	Z2	Z3	Z4	Z5

			Z1	Z2	Z3	Z4	Z5
Summary for the Week	Total Training Time (min):						
			%	%	%	%	
Year-to-Date Summary	Total Training Time (min):		Z1	Z2	Z3	Z4	Z5
			%	%	%	%	

Notes:

Key Workout Type	Averages	am Heart Rate	Body Weight/ Fat	Recovery Heart Rate	Weight Training Time	Stretching Time	A, B, C, F Training Rating	Σ HZT HZT Points
	AVERAGE OR TOTALS							
		BPM	LBS.	BPM	MIN.	MIN.	RATING	

otes:

WEEK 28 OF LOG PAGES

YEAR: _____

Date	Sport Activity	DST Distance	⏱ Time	Time In Zone Z1	Z2	Z3	Z4	Z5

Summary for the Week	Total Training Time (min):	Z1	Z2	Z3	Z4	Z5
		%	%	%	%	%

Year-to-Date Summary	Total Training Time (min):	Z1	Z2	Z3	Z4	Z5
		%	%	%	%	%

Notes:

Key Workout Type	Averages	am Heart Rate	Body Weight/ Fat	Recovery Heart Rate	Weight Training Time	Stretching Time	A, B, C, F Training Rating	Σ HZT HZT Points
		AVERAGE OR TOTALS						
		BPM	LBS.	BPM	MIN.	MIN.	RATING	

otes:

4 WEEK BLOCK

SUMMARY

4 Week Block: 7	Total Year-to-Date
Sport:	
Sport:	
Sport:	

Total Distance: _____ Year-to-Date _____

Total Time: _____ Year-to-Date _____

# of Key Workouts: _____ Year-to-Date _____

Total Time in Each Heart Zone:

• Zone 1 Healthy Heart _____

• Zone 2 Temperate _____

• Zone 3 Aerobic _____

• Zone 4 Threshold _____

• Zone 5 Red Line _____

Goals Accomplished This Month:

1. _____

2. _____

3. _____

4. _____

Goals to be Accomplished Next Month:

1. _____

2. _____

3. _____

4. _____

4 WEEK BLOCK
SUMMARY

Comments about my physical training:

_____
_____
_____
_____

Comments about my emotional training:

_____
_____
_____
_____

Comments about my overall training:

_____
_____
_____
_____

Date	Sport Activity	DST Distance	⏱ Time	Z1	Z2	⏱ Time In Zone Z3	Z4	Z5
Summary for the Week	Total Training Time (min):			Z1	Z2 %	Z3 %	Z4 %	Z5 %
Year-to-Date Summary	Total Training Time (min):			Z1	Z2 %	Z3 %	Z4 %	Z5 %

Notes:

Key Workout Type	Averages	am Heart Rate	Body Weight/ Fat	Recovery Heart Rate	Weight Training Time	Stretching Time	A, B, C, F Training Rating	Σ HZT HZT Points
		A V E R A G E		O R		T O T A L S		
		BPM	LBS.	BPM	MIN.	MIN.	RATING	

Notes:

Date	Sport Activity	DST Distance	Time	Time In Zone Z1	Z2	Z3	Z4	Z5

Summary for the Week	Total Training Time (min):	Z1	Z2	Z3	Z4	Z5
		%	%	%	%	
Year-to-Date Summary	Total Training Time (min):	Z1	Z2	Z3	Z4	Z5
		%	%	%	%	

Notes:

Key Workout Type	Averages	am Heart Rate	Body Weight/ Fat	Recovery Heart Rate	Weight Training Time	Stretching Time	A, B, C, F Training Rating	Σ HZT HZT Points
		A V E R A G E	O R	T O T A L S				
		BPM	LBS.	BPM	MIN.	MIN.	RATING	

Notes:

Date	Sport Activity	DST Distance	Time	Time In Zone Z1	Z2	Z3	Z4	Z5
Summary for the Week	Total Training Time (min):			Z1	Z2	Z3	Z4	Z5
				%	%	%	%	
Year-to-Date Summary	Total Training Time (min):			Z1	Z2	Z3	Z4	Z5
				%	%	%	%	

Notes:

Key Workout Type	Averages	am Heart Rate	Body Weight/ Fat	Recovery Heart Rate	Weight Training Time	STRETCH Stretching Time	A, B, C, F Training Rating	Σ HZT HZT Points
			A V E R A G E O R T O T A L S					
		BPM	LBS.	BPM	MIN.	MIN.	RATING	

tes:

Date	Sport Activity	DST Distance	Time	Z1	Z2	Z3	Z4	Z5

Time In Zone

Summary for the Week	Total Training Time (min):			Z1	Z2	Z3	Z4	Z5
					%	%	%	%
Year-to-Date Summary	Total Training Time (min):			Z1	Z2	Z3	Z4	Z5
					%	%	%	%

Notes:

Key Workout Type	Averages	am Heart Rate	Body Weight/ Fat	Recovery Heart Rate	Weight Training Time	STRETCH Stretching Time	A, B, C, F Training Rating	Σ HZT HZT Points
	A V E R A G E O R T O T A L S							
		BPM	LBS.	BPM	MIN.	MIN.	RATING	

otes:

4 WEEK BLOCK
SUMMARY

4 Week Block: 8	Total Year-to-Date
Sport:	
Sport:	
Sport:	

Total Distance: _____ Year-to-Date _____

Total Time: _____ Year-to-Date _____

# of Key Workouts: _____ Year-to-Date _____

Total Time in Each Heart Zone:

• Zone 1 Healthy Heart _____

• Zone 2 Temperate _____

• Zone 3 Aerobic _____

• Zone 4 Threshold _____

• Zone 5 Red Line _____

Goals Accomplished This Month:

1. _____

2. _____

3. _____

4. _____

Goals to be Accomplished Next Month:

1. _____

2. _____

3. _____

4. _____

4 WEEK BLOCK
SUMMARY

Comments about my physical training:

_____

_____

_____

_____

Comments about my emotional training:

_____

_____

_____

_____

Comments about my overall training:

_____

_____

_____

_____

Date	Sport Activity	DST Distance	Time	Time In Zone				
				Z1	Z2	Z3	Z4	Z5

Summary for the Week	Total Training Time (min):	Z1	Z2	Z3	Z4	Z5
		%	%	%	%	
Year-to-Date Summary	Total Training Time (min):	Z1	Z2	Z3	Z4	Z5
		%	%	%	%	

Notes:

Key Workout Type	Averages	am Heart Rate	Body Weight/ Fat	Recovery Heart Rate	Weight Training Time	Stretching Time	A, B, C, F Training Rating	Σ HZT HZT Points
		A V E R A G E	O R	T O T A L S				
		BPM	LBS.	BPM	MIN.	MIN.	RATING	

tes:

Date	Sport Activity	DST Distance	Time	Z1	Z2	Z3	Z4	Z5

		Z1	Z2	Z3	Z4	Z5
Summary for the Week	Total Training Time (min):					
		%	%	%	%	
Year-to-Date Summary	Total Training Time (min):	Z1	Z2	Z3	Z4	Z5
		%	%	%	%	

Notes:

Key Workout Type	Averages	am Heart Rate	Body Weight/ Fat	Recovery Heart Rate	Weight Training Time	STRETCH Stretching Time	A, B, C, F Training Rating	Σ HZT HZT Points
	A V E R A G E			O R		T O T A	L S	
		BPM	LBS.	BPM	MIN.	MIN.	RATING	

Notes:

WEEK 35 OF LOG PAGES

YEAR: _____

Date	Sport Activity	DST Distance	Time	Z1	Z2	Z3	Z4	Z5

Time In Zone

Summary for the Week	Total Training Time (min):	Z1	Z2	Z3	Z4	Z5
		%	%	%	%	
Year-to-Date Summary	Total Training Time (min):	Z1	Z2	Z3	Z4	Z5
		%	%	%	%	

Notes:

Key Workout Type	Averages	am Heart Rate	Body Weight/ Fat	Recovery Heart Rate	Weight Training Time	Stretching Time	A, B, C, F Training Rating	Σ HZT HZT Points
	AVERAGE OR TOTALS							
		BPM	LBS.	BPM	MIN.	MIN.	RATING	

tes:

Date	Sport Activity	DST Distance	Time	Z1	Z2	Z3	Z4	Z5
Summary for the Week	Total Training Time (min):			Z1	Z2	Z3	Z4	Z5
				%	%	%	%	
Year-to-Date Summary	Total Training Time (min):			Z1	Z2	Z3	Z4	Z5
				%	%	%	%	

Notes:

Key Workout Type	Averages	am Heart Rate	Body Weight/ Fat	Recovery Heart Rate	Weight Training Time	Stretching Time	A, B, C, F Training Rating	Σ HZT HZT Points
	A V E R A G E O R T O T A L S							
		BPM	LBS.	BPM	MIN.	MIN.	RATING	

Notes:

4 WEEK BLOCK
SUMMARY

4 Week Block: 9	Total Year-to-Date
Sport:	
Sport:	
Sport:	

Total Distance: _____ Year-to-Date _____

Total Time: _____ Year-to-Date _____

# of Key Workouts: _____ Year-to-Date _____

Total Time in Each Heart Zone:

• Zone 1 Healthy Heart _____

• Zone 2 Temperate_____

• Zone 3 Aerobic _____

• Zone 4 Threshold_____

• Zone 5 Red Line _____

Goals Accomplished This Month:

1. _____

2. _____

3. _____

4. _____

Goals to be Accomplished Next Month:

1. _____

2. _____

3. _____

4. _____

4 WEEK BLOCK
SUMMARY

Comments about my physical training:

_____

_____

_____

_____

Comments about my emotional training:

_____

_____

_____

_____

Comments about my overall training:

_____

_____

_____

_____

Date	Sport Activity	DST Distance	Time	Z1	Z2	Z3	Z4	Z5

Time In Zone

Summary for the Week	Total Training Time (min):			Z1	Z2	Z3	Z4	Z5
				%	%	%	%	

Year-to-Date Summary	Total Training Time (min):			Z1	Z2	Z3	Z4	Z5
				%	%	%	%	

Notes:

Key Workout Type	Averages	am Heart Rate	Body Weight/ Fat	Recovery Heart Rate	Weight Training Time	Stretching Time	A, B, C, F Training Rating	∑ HZT HZT Points
			A V E R A G E O R T O T A L S					
		BPM	LBS.	BPM	MIN.	MIN.	RATING	

Notes:

Date	Sport Activity	DST Distance	Time	Z1	Z2	Z3	Z4	Z5
Summary for the Week	Total Training Time (min):			Z1	Z2	Z3	Z4	Z5
					%	%	%	%
Year-to-Date Summary	Total Training Time (min):			Z1	Z2	Z3	Z4	Z5
					%	%	%	%

Notes:

Key Workout Type	Averages	am Heart Rate	Body Weight/ Fat	Recovery Heart Rate	Weight Training Time	Stretching Time	A, B, C, F Training Rating	Σ HZT HZT Points
	A V E R A G E	O R	T O T A L S					
		BPM	LBS.	BPM	MIN.	MIN.	RATING	

Notes:

Date	Sport Activity	DST Distance	Time	Time In Zone				
				Z1	Z2	Z3	Z4	Z5
Summary for the Week	Total Training Time (min):			Z1	Z2	Z3	Z4	Z5
				%	%	%	%	
Year-to-Date Summary	Total Training Time (min):			Z1	Z2	Z3	Z4	Z5
				%	%	%	%	

Notes:

Key Workout Type	Averages	am Heart Rate	Body Weight/ Fat	Recovery Heart Rate	Weight Training Time	Stretching Time	A, B, C, F Training Rating	Σ HZT HZT Points
		A V E R A G E O R T O T A L S						
		BPM	LBS.	BPM	MIN.	MIN.	RATING	

Notes:

WEEK 40 OF LOG PAGES

YEAR: _____

Date	Sport Activity	DST Distance	Time	Z1	Z2	Z3	Z4	Z5

Time In Zone (Z1–Z5 headers)

Summary for the Week	Total Training Time (min):			Z1	Z2	Z3	Z4	Z5
				%	%	%	%	%

Year-to-Date Summary	Total Training Time (min):			Z1	Z2	Z3	Z4	Z5
				%	%	%	%	%

Notes:

Key Workout Type	Averages	am Heart Rate	Body Weight/ Fat	Recovery Heart Rate	Weight Training Time	Stretching Time	A, B, C, F Training Rating	Σ HZT HZT Points
		A V E R A G E O R T O T A L S						
		BPM	LBS.	BPM	MIN.	MIN.	RATING	

Notes:

4 WEEK BLOCK

SUMMARY

4 Week Block: 10	Total Year-to-Date
Sport:	
Sport:	
Sport:	

Total Distance: _____ Year-to-Date _____

Total Time: _____ Year-to-Date _____

# of Key Workouts: _____ Year-to-Date _____

Total Time in Each Heart Zone:

- Zone 1 Healthy Heart _____
- Zone 2 Temperate_____
- Zone 3 Aerobic _____
- Zone 4 Threshold_____
- Zone 5 Red Line _____

Goals Accomplished This Month:

1. _____
2. _____
3. _____
4. _____

Goals to be Accomplished Next Month:

1. _____
2. _____
3. _____
4. _____

4 WEEK BLOCK
SUMMARY

Comments about my physical training:

_____

_____

_____

_____

Comments about my emotional training:

_____

_____

_____

_____

Comments about my overall training:

_____

_____

_____

_____

Date	Sport Activity	DST Distance	Time	Time In Zone Z1	Z2	Z3	Z4	Z5

Summary for the Week	Total Training Time (min):			Z1	Z2	Z3	Z4	Z5
				%	%	%	%	%
Year-to-Date Summary	Total Training Time (min):			Z1	Z2	Z3	Z4	Z5
				%	%	%	%	%

Notes:

Key Workout Type	Averages	am Heart Rate	Body Weight/ Fat	Recovery Heart Rate	Weight Training Time	Stretching Time	A, B, C, F Training Rating	Σ HZT HZT Points
	A V E R A G E O R T O T A L S							
		BPM	LBS.	BPM	MIN.	MIN.	RATING	

otes:

Date	Sport Activity	DST Distance	Time	Time In Zone Z1	Z2	Z3	Z4	Z5

	Total Training Time (min):			Z1	Z2	Z3	Z4	Z5
Summary for the Week								
				%	%	%	%	%
Year-to-Date Summary	Total Training Time (min):			Z1	Z2	Z3	Z4	Z5
				%	%	%	%	%

Notes:

Key Workout Type	Averages	am Heart Rate	Body Weight/ Fat	Recovery Heart Rate	Weight Training Time	Stretching Time	A, B, C, F Training Rating	Σ HZT HZT Points
	A V E R A G E O R T O T A L S							
		BPM	LBS.	BPM	MIN.	MIN.	RATING	

Notes:

Date	Sport Activity	Distance	Time	Z1	Z2	Z3	Z4	Z5
	DST	Distance	Time	Time In Zone				
Summary for the Week	Total Training Time (min):			Z1	Z2	Z3	Z4	Z5
				%	%	%	%	%
Year-to-Date Summary	Total Training Time (min):			Z1	Z2	Z3	Z4	Z5
				%	%	%	%	%

Notes:

Key Workout Type	Averages	am Heart Rate	Body Weight/ Fat	Recovery Heart Rate	Weight Training Time	Stretching Time	A, B, C, F Training Rating	Σ HZT HZT Points
	A V E R A G E O R T O T A L S							
		BPM	LBS.	BPM	MIN.	MIN.	RATING	

Notes:

Date	Sport Activity	DST Distance	Time	Time In Zone Z1	Z2	Z3	Z4	Z5

Summary for the Week	Total Training Time (min):			Z1	Z2	Z3	Z4	Z5
				%	%	%	%	%

Year-to-Date Summary	Total Training Time (min):			Z1	Z2	Z3	Z4	Z5
				%	%	%	%	%

Notes:

Key Workout Type	Averages	am Heart Rate	Body Weight/ Fat	Recovery Heart Rate	Weight Training Time	Stretching Time	A, B, C, F Training Rating	Σ HZT HZT Points
		A V E R A G E O R T O T A L S						
		BPM	LBS.	BPM	MIN.	MIN.	RATING	

Notes:

4 WEEK BLOCK

SUMMARY

4 Week Block: 11	Total Year-to-Date
Sport:	
Sport:	
Sport:	

Total Distance: _____ Year-to-Date _____

Total Time: _____ Year-to-Date _____

# of Key Workouts: _____ Year-to-Date _____

Total Time in Each Heart Zone:

- Zone 1 Healthy Heart _____
- Zone 2 Temperate _____
- Zone 3 Aerobic _____
- Zone 4 Threshold _____
- Zone 5 Red Line _____

Goals Accomplished This Month:

1. _____

2. _____

3. _____

4. _____

Goals to be Accomplished Next Month:

1. _____

2. _____

3. _____

4. _____

4 WEEK BLOCK
SUMMARY

Comments about my physical training:

_____

_____

_____

_____

Comments about my emotional training:

_____

_____

_____

_____

Comments about my overall training:

_____

_____

_____

_____

Date	Sport Activity	DST Distance	Time	Time In Zone				
				Z1	Z2	Z3	Z4	Z5
Summary for the Week	Total Training Time (min):			Z1	Z2	Z3	Z4	Z5
				%	%	%	%	%
Year-to-Date Summary	Total Training Time (min):			Z1	Z2	Z3	Z4	Z5
				%	%	%	%	%

Notes:

Key Workout Type	Averages	am Heart Rate	Body Weight/ Fat	Recovery Heart Rate	Weight Training Time	Stretching Time	A, B, C, F Training Rating	Σ HZT HZT Points
	AVERAGE OR TOTALS							
		BPM	LBS.	BPM	MIN.	MIN.	RATING	

Notes:

Date	Sport Activity	DST Distance	Time	Time In Zone				
				Z1	Z2	Z3	Z4	Z5

Summary for the Week	Total Training Time (min):			Z1	Z2	Z3	Z4	Z5
				%	%	%	%	%
Year-to-Date Summary	Total Training Time (min):			Z1	Z2	Z3	Z4	Z5
				%	%	%	%	%

Notes:

Key Workout Type	Averages	am Heart Rate	Body Weight/ Fat	Recovery Heart Rate	Weight Training Time	STRETCH Stretching Time	A, B, C, F Training Rating	Σ HZT HZT Points
	AVERAGE OR TOTALS							
		BPM	LBS.	BPM	MIN.	MIN.	RATING	

Notes:

Date	Sport Activity	DST Distance	⏱ Time	Z1	Time In Zone Z2	Z3	Z4	Z5
Summary for the Week	Total Training Time (min):			Z1 %	Z2 %	Z3 %	Z4 %	Z5
Year-to-Date Summary	Total Training Time (min):			Z1 %	Z2 %	Z3 %	Z4 %	Z5

Notes:

Key Workout Type	Averages	am Heart Rate	Body Weight/ Fat	Recovery Heart Rate	Weight Training Time	Stretching Time	A, B, C, F Training Rating	Σ HZT HZT Points
		AVERAGE OR TOTALS						
		BPM	LBS.	BPM	MIN.	MIN.	RATING	

tes:

Date	Sport Activity	DST Distance	Time	Z1	Z2	Z3	Z4	Z5

Time In Zone (columns Z1, Z2, Z3, Z4, Z5)

Summary for the Week	Total Training Time (min):	Z1	Z2	Z3	Z4	Z5
			%	%	%	%

Year-to-Date Summary	Total Training Time (min):	Z1	Z2	Z3	Z4	Z5
			%	%	%	%

Notes:

Key Workout Type	Averages	am Heart Rate	Body Weight/ Fat	Recovery Heart Rate	Weight Training Time	Stretching Time	A, B, C, F Training Rating	HZT Points
		A V E R A G E		O R	T O T A L S			
		BPM	LBS.	BPM	MIN.	MIN.	RATING	

Notes:

4 WEEK BLOCK
SUMMARY

4 Week Block: 12	Total Year-to-Date
Sport:	
Sport:	
Sport:	

Total Distance: _____ Year-to-Date _____

Total Time: _____ Year-to-Date _____

# of Key Workouts: _____ Year-to-Date _____

Total Time in Each Heart Zone:

- Zone 1 Healthy Heart _____
- Zone 2 Temperate _____
- Zone 3 Aerobic _____
- Zone 4 Threshold _____
- Zone 5 Red Line _____

Goals Accomplished This Month:

1. _____
2. _____
3. _____
4. _____

Goals to be Accomplished Next Month:

1. _____
2. _____
3. _____
4. _____

4 WEEK BLOCK
SUMMARY

Comments about my physical training:

_____

_____

_____

_____

Comments about my emotional training:

_____

_____

_____

_____

Comments about my overall training:

_____

_____

_____

_____

Date	Sport Activity	DST Distance	Time	Z1	Z2	Z3	Z4	Z5

		Z1	Z2	Z3	Z4	Z5
Summary for the Week	Total Training Time (min):					
		%	%	%	%	
Year-to-Date Summary	Total Training Time (min):	Z1	Z2	Z3	Z4	Z5
		%	%	%	%	

Notes:

Key Workout Type	Averages	am Heart Rate	Body Weight/ Fat	Recovery Heart Rate	Weight Training Time	Stretching Time	A, B, C, F Training Rating	HZT Points
		AVERAGE OR TOTALS						
		BPM	LBS.	BPM	MIN.	MIN.	RATING	

tes:

Date	Sport Activity	DST Distance	Time	Z1	Z2	Z3	Z4	Z5

Time In Zone

				Z1	Z2	Z3	Z4	Z5
Summary for the Week	Total Training Time (min):							
				%	%	%	%	
Year-to-Date Summary	Total Training Time (min):			Z1	Z2	Z3	Z4	Z5
				%	%	%	%	

Notes:

Key Workout Type	Averages	am Heart Rate	Body Weight/ Fat	Recovery Heart Rate	Weight Training Time	Stretching Time	A, B, C, F Training Rating	Σ HZT HZT Points
	A V E R A G E O R T O T A L S							
		BPM	LBS.	BPM	MIN.	MIN.	RATING	

tes:

WEEK 51 OF LOG PAGES

YEAR: _____

Date	Sport Activity	DST Distance	Time	Time In Zone Z1	Z2	Z3	Z4	Z5

Summary for the Week	Total Training Time (min):	Z1	Z2	Z3	Z4	Z5
		%	%	%	%	

Year-to-Date Summary	Total Training Time (min):	Z1	Z2	Z3	Z4	Z5
		%	%	%	%	

Notes:

Key Workout Type	Averages	am Heart Rate	Body Weight/ Fat	Recovery Heart Rate	Weight Training Time	STRETCH Stretching Time	A, B, C, F Training Rating	Σ HZT HZT Points
		A V E R A G E	O R	T O T A L S				
		BPM	LBS.	BPM	MIN.	MIN.	RATING	

Notes:

Date	Sport Activity	DST Distance	Time	Z1	Z2	Z3	Z4	Z5
Summary for the Week	Total Training Time (min):			Z1	Z2 %	Z3 %	Z4 %	Z5 %
Year-to-Date Summary	Total Training Time (min):			Z1	Z2 %	Z3 %	Z4 %	Z5 %

Notes:

Key Workout Type	Averages	am Heart Rate	Body Weight/ Fat	Recovery Heart Rate	Weight Training Time	Stretching Time	A, B, C, F Training Rating	Σ HZT HZT Points
	A V E R A G E O R T O T A L S							
		BPM	LBS.	BPM	MIN.	MIN.	RATING	

tes:

4 WEEK BLOCK
SUMMARY

4 Week Block: 13	Total Year-to-Date
Sport:	
Sport:	
Sport:	

Total Distance: _____ Year-to-Date _____

Total Time: _____ Year-to-Date _____

# of Key Workouts: _____ Year-to-Date _____

Total Time in Each Heart Zone:

- Zone 1 Healthy Heart _____
- Zone 2 Temperate _____
- Zone 3 Aerobic _____
- Zone 4 Threshold _____
- Zone 5 Red Line _____

Goals Accomplished This Month:

1. _____
2. _____
3. _____
4. _____

Goals to be Accomplished Next Month:

1. _____
2. _____
3. _____
4. _____

4 WEEK BLOCK
SUMMARY

Comments about my physical training:

_____

_____

_____

_____

Comments about my emotional training:

_____

_____

_____

_____

Comments about my overall training:

_____

_____

_____

_____

WEEK _____ OF LOG PAGES   YEAR: _____

Date	Sport Activity	DST Distance	Time	Z1	Z2	Z3	Z4	Z!

Time In Zone

Summary for the Week	Total Training Time (min):	Z1	Z2	Z3	Z4	Z5
		%	%	%	%	
Year-to-Date Summary	Total Training Time (min):	Z1	Z2	Z3	Z4	Z5
		%	%	%	%	

Notes:

Key orkout Type	Averages	am Heart Rate	Body Weight/ Fat	Recovery Heart Rate	Weight Training Time	Stretching Time	A, B, C, F Training Rating	Σ HZT HZT Points
		A V E R A G E O R T O T A L S						
		BPM	LBS.	BPM	MIN.	MIN.	RATING	

tes:

ANNUAL
SUMMARY CHART

Month	Number of Workouts	Total Distance/ Time	Total Heart Zone Training Points
1			
2			
3			
4			
5			
6			
7			
8			
9			
10			
11			
12			

RECORD OF
EVENTS & RACES

Date	Name of Event/Race	Results

FIVE STEPS TO A SUCCESSFUL
TRAINING PROGRAM

If you are ready to learn more about training and to initiate your own written training program, there's a basic system to follow. It consists of the following steps:

Step 1. Getting Started by Thinking It Through

It's important to begin by carefully prioritizing your training goals, and determining how you will accomplish them and what is required to do so. Consider what you will need in terms of time. Then, think through your equipment needs and facilities required. Most critically, determine what motivates you by asking WIIFM, or "What's In It for Me?" Answer other important self-questions: Are you ready to make the commitment required? How do you plan to fit your training into your present lifestyle? What changes are required? What methods have helped you achieve your goals in the past, and how can you incorporate them into your training plan? The better your self-assessment at this point, the better your start on a productive training program.

Step 2. Take Self Tests

This is an evaluation process to determine your current level of fitness. The only way to know if you are getting fitter and accomplishing your goals is to set some benchmarks, to evaluate your present physical condition. To start, here are three different self-tests in the three sports of triathlon – swim, bike, and run. Before you take these tests, make sure that you are at a comfortable base level of training. Each of the three different tests, which are a 1.5 mile run, a 400 yard swim, and a 3 mile ride, require an all out speed effort.

Take the tests on different days to allow adequate rest between each so that you can perform at your best. Then, using the Self-test Scorecard in this log book, determine whether you fall into a high, medium, or low fitness category, according to your performance in each activity. Repeat these tests on a regular basis to measure improved performance.

Step 3. Analyze Your Scores

Your scores will help you construct your basic training program. They will tell you which sport is your strongest and which needs the most improvement. As you train and continue to test yourself, these tests will be your reference point. If the scores increase, you will know that your training program is working. If your progress is minimal, then you will have to go back to the drawing board and rework your program.

Step 4. Set Your Training Goals

Now that you know where you stand – swim, bike and run, that is – you can begin to plan where you are going. Your primary goal will probably be to participate in and finish a triathlon or to better your last race time. To reach that goal you will need intermediate objectives. Be reasonable and be specific. Goal setting is not an easy task, but it can be simplified if you set down in writing in this log exactly what you want to accomplish.

The following section discusses goal-setting and gives you a place to record your short-term and long-term goals. Review your goals each month, in terms of what you have accomplished that month, and what you want to achieve the following month.

Step 5. You Can Do It

You have completed the other four steps: planning, self-testing, score analysis and goal setting. Now it is time to start your program. Use this log like a bible – it is a place to write down your workouts honestly – like a confessional. Refer back to prior weeks, keep your charts and graphs current and fill them out with joy and triumph. You are, you know, a multi-fit human. Train with both your heart and mind and you will be successful.

ANNUAL
GOALS

Writing down your training goals is a process. In a simplified form, here is a way to determine some training goals.

You have committed to training because you want to accomplish something. What is it that you want? Answer the question *Why am I training or thinking about starting a training program?* You probably have more than one goal. One of the first steps is to write down your personal exercise or training goals and then design a workout plan to attain them.

Most individuals exercise not because they love to, but because they want something out of it – to get healthier, fitter, and/or to perform better. But, you must be specific here and write down both your short term (for the next three months), and long-term goals. Set some target dates. The more quantitative you are the better your chances of accomplishing your goals.

Training means exercising with a goal in mind. Exercise is working out for the joy of the workout, or just to pass time.

Follow the WIIFM principle. That is, answer the question, "**W**hat's **I**n **I**t **F**or **M**e?" When you know what you want, it's easier to design a path to get there. Keep your goals simple, measurable, within reach, timely, and accountable.

Short-Term Training Goals:

1. _____
   _____
   _____

2. _____
   _____
   _____

3. _____
   _____
   _____

Long-Term Training Goals:

1. _____
   _____
   _____

2. _____
   _____
   _____
   _____

3. _____
   _____
   _____
   _____

TEN TYPES OF
WORKOUTS

Every triathlete knows that top performance must be achieved by developing a varied program that builds to peak conditioning. To reach that point, there are ten training regimes that can be used to enhance a total fitness system.

In nearly 30 years of training, I have followed these ten training types. They have served me well and helped me to reach the levels of athletic excellence that I have achieved and continue to help me in my daily workouts. I know that they will serve you well.

Sally Edwards
member of the Triathlon Hall of Fame

1. FARTLEK or SPEED PLAY: a method that involves varying the pace from a very slow jog to a high-speed run in continuous fashion. The pace changes at your will and typically does not relate to the distance of the run or the time, but to enjoyment.

2. LFD or LONG FAST DISTANCE: high intensity training of long duration, usually without rest intervals. The pace is equal to or faster than race pace and typically at or above anaerobic threshold levels.

3. INTERVALS: shorter, harder bouts of a specified distance, with a specified rest between repetitions, always done on a measured course. Always use heart rate as a measure of intensity.

4. SURGE TRAINING: a technique designed to prepare the triathlete for pace changes during the race. It is a combination of continuous race work pace with speed surges for specified distances.

5. REPETITION TRAINING: workouts of a given distance at a fast speed, usually close to race pace with long rest intervals to allow complete recovery of cardiac and respiratory systems.

6. LSD or LONG SLOW DISTANCE: easy workouts that approximate the distance of long races at below race intensity levels. (See Long Fast Distance)

7. OVER DISTANCE TRAINING: workouts that are longer than race distances which train the body to become comfortable with the duration of the event more than its intensity.

8. D.I.R.T. TRAINING: means Distances, Intervals, Repetitions, and Time and is a workout that includes all four of these training types in one workout.

9. RESISTANCE TRAINING: a workout that involves applying additional or opposing forces such as hills for running and biking or weight in swimming.

10. BRICKS: a workout in which you bike then run to train muscle groups to respond to racing conditions. An example is to complete a bike workout and immediately go for a short run without resting. It's a good workout to practice transition times.

DEFINITIONS

The word **"triathlon"** is spelled and pronounced with only one **"a"** not two as in **"triathalon".** Here is a list of ten key words used in the sport of triathlon that will help you not only swim, bike and run, but also speak the tri tongue.

Triathlon (tri ath lon) n. 1. Any event which combines the three sports of swimming, cycling, and running in any order. 2. A multisport activity of varying distances in which each contestant takes part in three events or stages which are either continuously timed or staged with interval periods between the events. Note: sometimes mispronounced triath-a-lon.

Cross Train (kros train) n. 1. A method of training in which the synergistic effects of one physical activity or physical conditioning regimen positively affect those of another. 2. A method of developing total fitness.

Triathlete (tri ath lete) n. 1. A person who trains and/or competes in the sport of triathlon. 2. Specifically, a person who participates in swimming, cycling, and running. (Antonym: single sport specialist)

Short Course Triathlon n. 1. A sprint triathlon. 2. A race in which the swim is less than 2 k, bike is less than 20 k and the run is less than 10 k in length.

DEFINITIONS

International Triathlon n. 1. A middle distance triathlon. 2. A triathlon in which the distances are exactly 1.5 k swim, 40 k bike and 10 k run.

Long Course Triathlon n. 1. A triathlon which is longer than the distances set at the international distance triathlons but shorter in length than ultra-distance races.

Ultra Distance Triathlon n. 1. The longest distance triathlon. 2. Usually considered to be Ironman distances of 2.4 mile swim, 112 mile bike, 26.2 mile marathon. 3. Races that can be longer than Ironman distances.

Duathlon (doo ath lon) n. A multi-sport event which includes only two events like run-bike-run.

Ironwoman / Ironman (i ern woom en) n. 1. A woman or man who competes in the trademarked international event called the Ironman. 2. Sometimes used to refer to a triathlete who competes in ultra distance events.

USING YOUR SELF - TEST
SCORECARD
FOR TRAINING

As you train, it is important to measure your improvements. Are you getting fitter? Are you getting faster? Are you experiencing the "positive training effect" which means that you physiology is responding by improved performance or the "negative training effect" which means you are becoming less fit.

Your Self-Test Scorecard is a benchmarking tool. By weekly taking at least one of the self-tests you can measure your progress. Do not do all the tests on the same day. Rather, take one every other day or one per week and note the results in this log. Using the scorecard, determine whether you fall into a high, medium or low category for each sport according to your results in each sport. Repeat these tests through your training on a regular basis to measure improved performance. Your numbers improve as you get fitter.

FOR EXAMPLE

You start a new training program and you score low on the run, medium on the swim, and high on the bike. Since triathlon is a three-legged stool – which means that if you have two short legs the stool doesn't sit straight. Adjust your training plan to focus on the run first because it is your lowest score Give attention to the bike, too. In the run you scored the highest so consider modifying your training by reducing your training load in the run and increasing the workouts in the other two sports.

SELF - TEST
SCORECARD

Fitness Categories	1 1/2 Mile RUN		400 Yard SWIM		3 Mile BIKE RIDE	
	Time	Score	Time	Score	Time	Score
High	7.05	20.0	5.01	20.0	5.53	20.0
	7.20	19.5	5.07	19.5	6.00	19.5
	7.35	19.0	5.13	19.0	6.08	19.0
	7.55	18.5	5.20	18.5	6.17	18.5
	8.05	18.0	5.27	18.0	6.26	18.0
	8.20	17.5	5.34	17.5	6.35	17.5
	8.35	17.0	5.41	17.0	6.45	17.0
	8.55	16.5	5.49	16.5	6.55	16.5
	9.10	16.0	5.57	16.0	7.05	16.0
	9.31	15.5	6.05	15.5	7.17	15.5
	9.50	15.0	6.14	15.0	7.29	15.0
	10.16	14.5	6.23	14.5	7.41	14.5
Medium	10.35	14.0	6.32	14.0	7.54	14.0
	11.01	13.5	6.42	13.5	8.08	13.5
	11.31	13.0	6.53	13.0	8.23	13.0
	12.01	12.5	7.04	12.5	8.39	12.5
	12.35	12.0	7.16	12.0	8.56	12.0
	13.10	11.5	7.28	11.5	9.14	11.5
	13.50	11.0	7.41	11.0	9.33	11.0
	14.31	10.5	7.55	10.5	9.54	10.5
	15.20	10.0	8.10	10.0	10.16	10.0
	16.10	9.5	8.26	9.5	10.40	9.5
Low	17.16	9.0	8.43	9.0	11.05	9.0
	18.25	8.5	9.01	8.5	11.33	8.5
	19.40	8.0	9.20	8.0	12.04	8.0
	21.16	7.5	9.41	7.5	12.37	7.5
	23.00	7.0	10.03	7.0	13.13	7.0
	25.00	6.5	10.27	6.5	13.53	6.5
	30.00	6.0	10.53	6.0	14.37	6.0
	32.00	5.5	11.21	5.5	15.26	5.5
	34.00	5.0	11.52	5.0	16.21	5.0
	36.00	4.5	12.25	4.5	17.07	4.5
	37.00	4.0	13.02	4.0	18.00	4.0

THE EASY-MODERATE HARD SUB-MAX TEST

To set your five different training zones in the Heart Zones Training system, you must measure your maximum heart rate. There are two ways to measure it: take a maximum heart rate test to the point of exhaustion or take a lower intensity sub-maximum test and estimate closely your maximum heart rate. You may not be ready or it may not be appropriate for you to take a maximum heart rate test. I recommend that you take a test that is sub- or below your maximum heart rate and estimate your true maximum heart rate.

There is no arithmetic formula that is accurate enough to use to measure your maximum heart rate. The old one that you may be familiar with is not based on any valid scientific evidence and is inaccurate. At Heart Zones, we have 8-10 different sub-max tests that you can teach, each takes from 3-10 minutes. We recommend that you take them all and average the results for the highest level of accuracy. You can learn more about all of the sub-maximum tests on our website www.heartzones.com.

One of the Heart Zones sub-max tests is called "Easy-Moderate-Hard Sub Max Text". This test as the title suggests, gives you low, moderate, and higher intensities that can be used to estimate your true maximum heart rate. Complete the "Easy-Moderate-Hard" test and score your results. Next, set your five heart zones using the Heart Zones Maximum Heart Rate chart in this log book. Always, train in the right zones to get the most benefits.

HOW TO CHOOSE A HEART RATE MONITOR

Purchasing a heart rate monitor is a lot like making the buying decisions about any electronic device – computer, PDA, or mobile phone. When you begin the shopping quest, you need to decide on what functions, the internal operating activities, of the monitor that you choose. You also need to decide on what features, the external operating activities that work for you.

First, you decide on what your needs and wants might be by answering the questions that follow. Second, go to the "Heart Rate Monitor BUYERS Chart" below and circle the functions and features that match your need and wants. Finally, go to our website: www.heartzones.com and find the monitor that meets those specifications and fits your budget.

TO BEGIN, ANSWER THESE QUESTIONS:

- What features do I need now?
- What functions do I need now?
- How may my needs grow?
- What is my budget?
- How much memory and programming of the monitor am I willing to do?
- Are maintenance, repair, and warranty issues important?
- Do I need to download my data into a computer or do I want playback the data on the monitor?
- Am I the kind of person who wants a plug-and-play monitor with one or less buttons because I just want to put it on and use it without programming the monitor before each workout?
- Am I going to take the time to learn how to use my monitor, to read the User's Guide, and enjoy information like recovery heart rate, time in zones, heart zones points, or heart rate lap data?
- Am I a gadget gal or guy who loves all of the bells and whistles of this personal training tool?

Today, there are nearly 200 different models and over 20 manufacturers of heart rate monitors. Each monitor has different functions and features. Each monitor requires unique programming or "button pushing". As you add more functions and features to the monitor, you add cost to the tool. As with other electronic products, monitors are going through the "convergence technology" product cycle. For example, you can get a cell phone or a PDA that also has heart rate as a function.

There are two different kinds of downloadable monitors: manual and computer based. Computer-based downloading of workout data into a heart rate workout profile and summary information can be one of the most interesting features of a training monitor. This output data is invaluable in measuring fitness improvement and permanently recording your workout sessions. It allows you to save the stored data for post-exercise time interpretation and evaluation. It provides validation, quantification, summary data of time in zones and heart zones training points, a measurement of training load. Manual downloading requires that you enter the data manually into your log or a computer spreadsheet.

What is most important is that a heart rate monitor is not a pedometer that works on the wrist and that tells you how fast your heart is beating. Rather, it is several devices all packaged into a personal training tool. If you are using the monitor that meets your needs, wants, and budget, you will find no better aid and supporter than your personal training tool – your heart rate number. Get ready. You are about to experience a new way to train with the potential to change the way you workout – emotionally and physically.

WATCH FUNCTION	HEAR RATE FUNCTIONS	RECORDING FUNCTION	TYPES OF DOWNLOADABLE MONITORS	TYPES OF TRANSMISSION	TYPES OF MONITORS	FEATURES
TIME OF DAY	CURRENT HEART RATE	PEAK HEART RATE	MANUAL RECALL	DIGITAL	CYCLING MONITORS*	REPLACEABLE BATTERY
STOPWATCH	ZONE ALARM: AUDIBLE OR VISUAL	TIME IN MULTIPLE ZONES	INFRARED	ANALOG	HORSE MONITORS	NO CHEST STRAP REQUIRED
WAKE UP ALARM	CEILING AND FLOORS SETTING	ESTIMATE: FAT BURNIING	SONIC LINK	CODED ANALOG	WEIGHT LOSS MONITORS	WATERPROOF
COUNT-DOWN TIMER	TIME IN ZONE(S) MEMORY	TIME ABOVE 1 ZONE	INTERFACE BOX	INFRARED	FITNESS MONITORS	MULTIPLE DISPLAY OPTIONS
COUNT-UP TIMER	AVERAGE HEART RATE	TIME BELOW 1 ZONE	TWO WAY LINKING		SWIMMING MONITORS	EASY TO READ DIGITS
BACKLIGHTING	PEAK HEART RATE	LAP(S) TIMING WITH HEART RATE**			STRESS MONITORS	WIRELESS TRANSMISSION
CALENDAR	WITHIN ZONE BAR	TOTAL EXERCISE TIME			ATHLETE'S MONITORS	TOGGLE BETWEEN AUDIBLE/SILENT ALARM MODES
WATER RESISTANT	CALORIE ESTIMA-TION, CUMULATIVE CALORIES	DISPLAY WORKOUT RESULTS AS BAR GRAPH OR PROFILE GRAPH			MOTIVATION MONITORS	COMFORTABLE AND COSMETIC DESIGNS
SINGLE AND CUMULATIVE EXERCISE TIME	HEART ZONE ESTIMATION	INTERVAL SETTINGS WITH AND WITHOUT HEART RATE			RUNNER'S MONITORS	BACKLIGHTING
	OXYGEN CONSUMPTION ESTIMATION	RECORDING RATES FOR HEART RATE SAMPLES				FITNESS TESTS
	RECOVERY FEATURES	MEMORY TIME INTERVAL SETTINGS (5, 30, 60 SECS)				USER'S PERSONAL INFORMATION: ID, NAME, LOGO
	SWITCH FUNCTION MODE BY TOUCH TO TRANSMITTER	RECORDING ALTITUDES				MEASUREMENT UNITS
	SUM OF TRAINING LOAD (HZT POINTS)	DYNAMIC MEMORY STORES AND DISPLAYS THE LAST FEW WORKOUTS				DISPLAY OPTIONS
	% OF MAXIMUM HEART RATE					UPLOAD DATA AND SETTING
						EASE OF PROGRAMMING WITH DISPLAY POINTERS OR TEXT
						HELP KEY
						DISTANCE WALK/ RUN+ HEART RATE
						ZOOM WHICH ENLARGES THE DATA IN THE DISPLAY

* Cycling monitors feature speed, altitude, thermometer, cadence, riding time, and power output.

** Lap time may include: best lap time/lap and split times, current, average and peak heart rate for each lap, cycling samples saved at the preset recording intervals (5, 30, 60 secs); and other information at the end of each lap.

HEART ZONES® TRAINING — THE ZONES CHART ©

ZONE	MAXIMUM HEART RATE	FUEL BURNED* (per min)	CALORIES BURNED* (Cal/min)* (Cal/30min)	WORKOUT TYPE	BENEFITS	HZT POINTS°	WELLNESS ZONES	LACTATE * CONCENTRATION	VO₂§	RATING OF PERCEIVED EXERTION	DESCRIPTION OF RPE	TALK
5 REDLINE RED ZONE	100% ↕ 90%		~20 Cal/min ~600	Max effort, sprinting, high speed intervals	Improved lactate tolerance **GET FASTEST**	×5	PERFORMANCE ZONES	>8 mmol/L	100 ↕ 83	10 ↕ 7	maximal effort to very, very hard	Can't talk except for very short phrases
4 THRESHOLD ORANGE ZONE	90% ↕ 80%		~15 Cal/min ~450	Time trials, intervals, tempo, hill work	Improved anaerobic capacity, lactate clearance **GET FASTER**	×4		4-8 mmol/L	83 ↕ 70	7 ↕ 5	very, very hard to hard	Can still talk, but not comfortably
3 AEROBIC YELLOW ZONE	80% ↕ 70%		~10 Cal/min ~300	Endurance and steady-state	Improved aerobic capacity, optimal cardiovascular training **GET FITTER**	×3	FITNESS ZONES	3-4 mmol/L	70 ↕ 58	5 ↕ 4	hard to somewhat hard	Very aware of breathing, still comfortable to talk
2 TEMPERATE GREEN ZONE	70% ↕ 60%		~7 Cal/min ~210	LSD (long slow distance), recovery and regeneration	Improved fat mobilization basic cardio training **STAY FIT**	×2		2-3 mmol/L	58 ↕ 39	4 ↕ 2.5	somewhat hard to easy	Aware of breathing, very comfortable talking
1 HEALTHY HEART BLUE ZONE	60% ↕ 50%		~4 Cal/min ~120	Warm-up and cool-down rehabilitation	Improved self-esteem, stress reduction, blood chemistry **GET FIT**	×1	HEALTH ZONES	<2 mmol/L	39 ↕ 28	2.5 ↕ 1	easy to very easy	Easy conversation, just like sitting and talking

INTENSITY MEASUREMENTS

▢ amount of fat burned

▢ amount of carbohydrates burned

** In all zones, approximately 5% of the calories burned are protein which is negligible.

* Lactate is the concentration of lactic acid in the blood.

§ VO₂ is the amount or volume of oxygen used.

* Only an estimation, highly variable between individuals. Approximate for 150lb person, walking or running, 20-25% body fat.

HEART ZONES® TRAINING ⮫ MAXIMUM HEART RATE ©

Training Zone (% maximum heart rate)	Fuel Burned	160	165	170	175	180	185	190	195	200	205	210	215	220	225	230	235	240
Z5 RED LINE 90%-100%	PROTEIN → / CARBOHYDRATES / FAT	160	165	170	175	180	185	190	195	200	205	210	215	220	225	230	235	240
		144	149	153	158	162	167	171	176	180	185	189	194	198	203	207	211	216
Z4 THRESHOLD 80%-90%		144	149	153	158	162	167	171	176	180	185	189	194	198	203	207	211	216
		128	132	136	140	144	148	152	156	160	164	168	172	176	180	184	188	192
Z3 AEROBIC 70%-80%		128	132	136	140	144	148	152	156	160	164	168	172	176	180	184	188	192
		112	116	119	123	126	130	133	137	140	143	147	151	154	158	164	165	168
Z2 TEMPERATE 60%-70%		112	116	119	123	126	130	133	137	140	143	147	151	154	158	164	165	168
		96	99	102	105	108	111	114	117	120	123	126	129	132	135	138	141	144
Z1 HEALTHY HEART 50%-60%		96	99	102	105	108	111	114	117	120	123	126	129	132	135	138	141	144
		80	83	85	88	90	93	95	98	100	103	105	108	110	113	115	118	120

Emotional Heart Zones

ZONE NUMBER		EMOTIONAL ZONE	FEELING IN ZONE	HEALTH RESULTS
5		Red Zone	Out of Control, frantic, total panic, disconnected, emergency	Toxic, harms the health and safety of self and others. Body becomes "maladapted" to the stress response. Unhealthy weight gain or weight loss, susceptibility to mental disorders and addictions.
4		Distress Zone	Worried, anxious, angry, scattered, fearful, reactive	Elevated blood pressure, high cholesterol and increased risk of heart disease. Increased risk of infections, certain cancers, allergies and autoimmune diseases. Poor concentration. Increased muscular stress, Hormonal changes that result in weight gain, Increased risk of degenerative disease. Premature aging.
3		Performance Zone	Focused, in the flow, "in my element", positive stress	Heightened awareness and creativity, Heightened physical endurance and performance. Improved mental performance. Faster reaction time. Less potential for accidents. Inspire and energize those around you.
2		Productive Zone	High concentration, effective, prolific	Improved capacity for undertaking tasks involving mental or physical dexterity. Improved learning ability. Behavior has positive effects on those around you.
1		Safe Zone	Meditative, relaxed, affirming, regenerative, comfortable, compassionate, peaceful	Increased patience, caring, compassion, capacity for love. Lowered risk of hypertension, Type 2 diabetes, immune disorders and mental disorders. Increased capacity for dealing with pain. Decrease in occurrence of stress-related disorders. Reduced dependence on prescribed medicine.

What is the Heart Zones Training System?

We say, "The Heart Zones Training system uses your personal cardiac training ranges to define your individual training program for optimum health, emotional fitness, and high performance." But what does that mean? Let's take it step by step.

Heart Zones Training is based on science, research, experience, and the precept that there is no such thing as a one-size-fits-all, universal training program. Rather, to be effective, exercise must be tailored to fit each of us.

And that's just what Heart Zones Training provides—a completely personalized exercise program that works for anyone, of any age, of any current fitness level, performing any activities.
It works for a 20-year-old professional athlete, a 70-year-old wanting to improve strength, a 30-year-old who has never been fit, a 55-year-old fighting fat, or a 40-year-old who has become sedentary.

How can Heart Zones Training provides personal training programs for everyone? By teaching you how to notice and respond to your own personal biofeedback device—your heartbeat. Whether you take your pulse manually or, for far better accuracy, use some sort of tool (ranging from an inexpensive heart rate monitor to a top-of-the-line distance-and-speed+heart rate system), either way you will be in tune with what truly matters for every aspect of your wellness—your heart.

HEART ZONES®
TRAINING

Heart Zones Publishing books are available at special quantity discounts for bulk purchases for sales promotions, premiums, fund-raising, or educational use. Special books, or book excerpts, can also be created to fit specific needs upon request. For details, write or contact:
Heart Zones Marketing, 2636 Fulton Avenue Suite #100, Sacramento, CA 95821.

Heart Zones USA
2636 Fulton Avenue • Suite 100
Sacramento, California 95821 USA
www.heartzones.com   staff@heartzones.com